# First World War
## and Army of Occupation
# War Diary
## France, Belgium and Germany

60 DIVISION
Headquarters, Branches and Services
General Staff
1 November 1915 - 31 December 1915

WO95/3026/1

The Naval & Military Press Ltd
www.nmarchive.com
**Published in association with The National Archives**

Published by

## The Naval & Military Press Ltd

Unit 10 Ridgewood Industrial Park,

Uckfield, East Sussex,

TN22 5QE England

Tel: +44 (0) 1825 749494

www.naval-military-press.com

www.nmarchive.com

*This diary has been reprinted in facsimile from the original. Any imperfections are inevitably reproduced and the quality may fall short of modern type and cartographic standards.*

© **Crown Copyright**
**Images reproduced by permission of The National Archives, London, England, 2015.**

# Contents

| Document type | Place/Title | Date From | Date To |
|---|---|---|---|
| Heading | WO95/3026/1 | | |
| Heading | 60th Division General Staff 1915 Nov-Dec 1916 Jun-1916 Nov | | |
| Heading | War Diary of Headquarters 60th (London) Division From 1st November 1915 To 30th November 1915 (Volume 1) | | |
| War Diary | | 01/11/1915 | 06/12/1915 |
| War Diary | Stansted Abbots | 07/12/1915 | 11/12/1915 |
| War Diary | Buntingford | 13/12/1915 | 20/12/1915 |
| War Diary | Bishops Stortford | 20/12/1915 | 20/12/1915 |
| War Diary | Sawbridge Worth | 20/12/1915 | 20/12/1915 |
| War Diary | Hatfield Broad Oak | 20/12/1915 | 20/12/1915 |
| War Diary | Harlow | 20/12/1915 | 20/12/1915 |
| War Diary | Bishops Stortford | 20/12/1915 | 20/12/1915 |
| War Diary | Ware | 21/12/1915 | 22/12/1915 |
| War Diary | Stansted | 22/12/1915 | 22/12/1915 |
| War Diary | Saffron Walden | 22/12/1915 | 22/12/1915 |
| War Diary | Haverhill | 22/12/1915 | 22/12/1915 |
| War Diary | Bishops Stortford | 22/12/1915 | 22/12/1915 |
| War Diary | Stansted | 22/12/1915 | 22/12/1915 |
| War Diary | Bishops Stortford | 22/12/1915 | 22/12/1915 |
| War Diary | Dunmow | 23/12/1915 | 23/12/1915 |
| War Diary | Braintree | 23/12/1915 | 23/12/1915 |
| War Diary | Coggeshall | 23/12/1915 | 23/12/1915 |
| War Diary | Bishops Stortford | 24/12/1915 | 24/12/1915 |
| War Diary | Hadham Station | 24/12/1915 | 24/12/1915 |
| War Diary | Standon | 24/12/1915 | 24/12/1915 |
| War Diary | Buntingford | 24/12/1915 | 27/12/1915 |
| War Diary | Maple Avenue | 28/12/1915 | 28/12/1915 |
| War Diary | Bishops Stortford | 28/12/1915 | 28/12/1915 |
| War Diary | Hadham Hall | 28/12/1915 | 28/12/1915 |
| War Diary | Elsenham Hall | 28/12/1915 | 29/12/1915 |
| War Diary | Gosfield | 30/12/1915 | 30/12/1915 |
| War Diary | Stansted | 31/12/1915 | 31/12/1915 |
| War Diary | Saffron Walden | 31/12/1915 | 31/12/1915 |

WO 95/3026/1

# 60TH DIVISION

## GENERAL STAFF
### JUN - NOV 1916

1915 NOV & DEC
1916 JUN - 1916 NOV

TO SALONIKA

Confidential

War Diary of

Headquarters

60th (London) Division

from 1st November 1915 to 30th November 1915

(Volume 1)

Army Form C. 2118.

# WAR DIARY
of
# INTELLIGENCE SUMMARY

*(Erase heading not required.)*

"M G"

Instructions regarding War Diaries and Intelligence Summaries are contained in F. S. Regs., Part II. and the Staff Manual respectively. Title pages will be prepared in manuscript.

| Hour, Date, Place | Summary of Events and Information | Remarks and references to Appendices |
|---|---|---|
| November 1st | 2 Officers and 3 N.C.O's (Infantry) proceeded to Chelsea for Course of Instruction.<br>9 men (2 - R.E. and 7 - Infantry) proceeded to St. Albans for Course of Instruction in Cookery.<br>2 Officers and 1 N.C.O. (Infantry) proceeded to Bisley for Machine Gun Course.<br>24 N.C.O's proceeded to Hadham Hall for fourth Divisional Range-taking Course. | |
| November 2nd | 1 N.C.O. and 1 man (Infantry) proceeded to Victoria Park for Course of Instruction in Cookery.<br>3 Officers and 5 N.C.O's (Infantry and 1 N.C.O. Cyclist Co.) proceeded to Aldershot for Course of Instruction in Physical Training. | |
| November 3rd | 1 N.C.O. (R.E.) proceeded to Aldershot for Course of Instruction in Mounted Duties.<br>1 Officer and 2 N.C.O's (Infantry) proceeded to Godstone for Grenadier Course. | |
| November 4th | Divisional Tactical Exercise ( 179th and 180th Infantry Brigades with proportion of Artillery and Cyclists) carried out at Quendon. | |
| November 5th | Lieut. Col. Dunlop, G.S.O.1, held a conference with Yeomanry and Cyclist Co. on the subject of Co-operation of Cavalry and Cyclists. | |
| November 6th | 2 men proceeded to Whitechapel for Artillery Leather Stitching and Rivetting Course. | |
| November 7th | 4 Officers proceeded to Shoeburyness for Artillery Course.<br>3 Officers and 3 N.C.O's (R.E.) proceeded to Brightlingsea for Military Engineering Course.<br>Capt. Napier, G.S.O.2, proceeded on duty to Godstone Grenadier School. | |

Army Form C. 2118.

# WAR DIARY
# or
# INTELLIGENCE SUMMARY

*(Erase heading not required.)*

Instructions regarding War Diaries and Intelligence Summaries are contained in F.S. Regs., Part II. and the Staff Manual respectively. Title pages will be prepared in manuscript.

| Hour, Date, Place | Summary of Events and Information | Remarks and references to Appendices |
|---|---|---|
| November 8th | Lecture by Divisional Bombing Instructor to 180th Infantry Brigade. 5 Officersvand 5 N.C.O's (Infantry) proceeded to Ongar for Military Engineering Course. Lieut. Col. Dunlop, G.S.O.1, held a conference with Officers from R.A., 179th and 180th Infantry Brigades on the subject "Ammunition Supply in the Field". G.O.C. held conference on Tactical Exercise held on 4th November. 1 Officer proceeded to Lark Hill, Salisbury Plain, for Course of Instruction in 4.5" Howitzer. 6 Officers and 10 N.C.O's (Infantry) proceed at Third Army Trench Fighting School at Kelvedon. 24 N.C.O's and men proceeded to Saddlery Class at Bishop's Stortford. Third Divisional Machine Gun Course of Instruction commenced at Hadham Hall. Fifth Divisional Range-taking Course commenced at Hadham Hall. | |
| November 12th | Lecture by Divisional Bombing Instructor to 179th Infantry Brigade, Royal Engineers, and Cyclist Company. | |
| November 14th | 4 Officers proceeded to Woolwich for Artillery Course. | |
| November 15th | 2 Officers and 4 N.C.O's (Infantry) proceeded to Bisley for Musketry Course. Officers from all units, and 24 men proceeded to Bishop's Stortford for Farriery Course, for a period of 3 days each. 1 Officer (Yeomanry) proceeded to Woolwich for Regimental Transport Officers Course. 6th Divisional Range-taking Course commenced at Hadham Hall. | |

# WAR DIARY or INTELLIGENCE SUMMARY

*(Erase heading not required.)*

Army Form C. 2118.

Instructions regarding War Diaries and Intelligence Summaries are contained in F. S. Regs., Part II. and the Staff Manual respectively. Title pages will be prepared in manuscript.

| Hour, Date, Place | Summary of Events and Information | Remarks and references to Appendices |
|---|---|---|
| November 16th | 2 Officers proceeded to Aldershot for A.S.C. Course. Lecture by Major Hutchison, General Staff, Third Army, to 181st Infantry Brigade, — "Occupation of Trenches and Reconnaissance Duties". | |
| November 17th | 15 Officers proceeded to Oxford for Elementary Course of Instruction. | |
| November 21st | 8 Officers proceeded to Dunstable for Artillery Signalling Course. 2 Officers and 3 N.C.O's (Infantry) proceeded to Godstone for Grenadier Course. | |
| November 22nd | Lecture by Divisional Bombing Instructor to 181st Infantry Brigade. 18 Officers proceeded to Cambridge for O.T.C. Course. 3 men proceeded to Colchester for Artillery Harness Repairing Course. 1 N.C.O. and 9 men (all units) proceeded to St. Albans for Course of Instruction in Cookery. 4 Officers and 2 N.C.O's proceeded to Bisley for Machine Gun Course. 1 Officer and 2 N.C.O's proceeded to Chelsea for Course of Instruction. 7th Divisional Range-taking Course commenced at Hadham Hall. | |
| November 23rd | Signal Company carried out 2 days' Exercise in Cable Laying. Signal Company Exercise – first day. | |
| November 24th | Signal Company Exercise – 2nd day. 3 Officers proceeded to Hertford for Junior Officers' Course. 6 Officers and 10 N.C.O's proceeded to Kelvedon for Course of Instruction at Third Army Trench Fighting School. | |
| November 25th | 5 Officers proceeded to Royal Military College, Camberley, for Officers' Course. | |
| November 26th | Lecture by Divisional Bombing Instructor to 180th Infantry Brigade. | |

Army Form C. 2118.

# WAR DIARY
## INTELLIGENCE SUMMARY
*(Erase heading not required.)*

Instructions regarding War Diaries and Intelligence Summaries are contained in F. S. Regs., Part II. and the Staff Manual respectively. Title pages will be prepared in manuscript.

| Hour, Date, Place | Summary of Events and Information | Remarks and references to Appendices |
|---|---|---|
| November 27th | 2 Officers proceeded to Edinburgh for Artillery Officers' Course. | |
| November 28th | 4 Officers proceeded to Woolwich for Artillery Course. | |
| November 29th | 1 N.C.O. and 6 men proceeded to Bermondsey for Course of Instruction in Cookery. 2/15th Battalion, London Regt. took over Firework Posts and Road Blocking duties from the detached Company of the 2/14th Battalion, London Regt. 4th Divisional Machine Gun Course commenced at Hadham Hall. 8th Divisional Range-taking Course commenced at Hadham Hall. | |
| November 30th | 1 N.C.O. proceeded to Aldershot for Course of Instruction in Physical Training. | |

Bishop's Stortford,
14th December 1915.

BRIGADIER-GENERAL,
Comdg. 60th (London) Division.

Army Form C. 2118.

# WAR DIARY
## or
## INTELLIGENCE SUMMARY.

(Erase heading not required.)

Instructions regarding War Diaries and Intelligence Summaries are contained in F.S. Regs., Part II. and the Staff Manual respectively. Title pages will be prepared in manuscript.

| Hour, Date, Place | Summary of Events and Information | Remarks and references to Appendices |
|---|---|---|
| 1st December 1915. | Letter received from III Army re system of Motor Buses for Columns of Supply and Ambulances on Emergency. (3A/CR/573/ST dated 30th November 1915.) | |
| 2nd " | Copy of above III Army letter, 3A/CR/573/ST of 30/11/15, sent to A.S.C. and "G" Branch. Remount Officers reports 50 L.D. Horses received. | |
| 3rd " | ............ | |
| 4th " | Copy of above III Army letter, 3A/CR/573/ST of 30/11/15, sent to 179th, 180th & 181st Infantry Brigades. | |
| 5th " | ............ | |
| 6th " | Secret letter to III Army (C/203/Q/100) forwarding acknowledgement of 3A/CR/573/ST dated 30th Nov.1915 re Motor Buses for Supply Columns and giving distribution - reporting all previous correspondence on the subject destroyed. | |
| 7th " | ............ | |
| 8th " | Remount Officer reports arrival of 50 H.D.Horses. | |
| 9th " | ............ | |
| 10th " | Remount Officers reports 45 H.D.Horses received. | |
| 11th " | ............ | |
| 12th " | ............ | |

Army Form C. 2118.

# WAR DIARY
## or
## INTELLIGENCE SUMMARY.
*(Erase heading not required.)*

Instructions regarding War Diaries and Intelligence Summaries are contained in F.S. Regs., Part II. and the Staff Manual respectively. Title pages will be prepared in manuscript.

| Hour, Date, Place | Summary of Events and Information | Remarks and references to Appendices |
|---|---|---|
| 13th December 1915. | Letter from D.B.O.Eastern Command pointing out correct method of procedure regarding payment of Sanitary Bills and sending to Eastern Command. Application made to III Army for short Carbines to be issued to Yeomanry in lieu of Rifles. | I.A. I.A. |
| 14th " | ............ | |
| 15th " | Orders issued that all places containing or that have recently contained horses with contagious disease to be labelled as such. Report asked for by III Army as to suitability of Mustard Straw for bedding purposes for horses. | I.A. I.A. |
| 16th " | ............ | |
| 17th " | ............ | |
| 18th " | ............ | |
| 19th " | ............ | |
| 20th " | Central Force (CR.CF.20275.OS) dated 20/12/15, two 15 pr.Dummies advised for Howitzer Bde. Letter to III Army stating .303" Arms received by Yeomanry and Divl.Cyclist Coy. | I.A. I.A. |
| 21st " | ............ | |
| 22nd " | Letter received from III Army (1724/ST dated 22/12/15) Bills arising out of Contracts to be forwarded to Eastern Command for approval. Remount Officer reports 22 Horses, various, received. Letter from III Army (1098/E dated 22nd Dec.) confirming action taken in regard to the repair of roads of 2/5th F.A.Brigade stables. | I.A. I.A. |
| 23rd " | Letter from III Army,(5698/ST of 22/12/15) forwarding two Circular Memos. from Central Force re initialling entries in A.B.383 also Supply Officers to state approx. quantity of straw and hay used to D.P.O.S. III Army ask for proposal for supply & transport for Artillery practice at LATCHINGDON PENINSULA. Central Force ask number of G.S.Wagons required to complete Division. | |

Army Form C. 2118.

# WAR DIARY
## or
## INTELLIGENCE SUMMARY.
*(Erase heading not required.)*

Instructions regarding War Diaries and Intelligence Summaries are contained in F.S. Regs., Part II. and the Staff Manual respectively. Title pages will be prepared in manuscript.

| Hour, Date, Place | Summary of Events and Information | Remarks and references to Appendices |
|---|---|---|
| 24th December 1915. | Letter from C.R.E.Colchester (39881 dated 23/12/15) stating D.O.R.E. will assist in work of repairs to Hut Stables. | I.A |
| 25th " | ......... | |
| 26th " | ......... | |
| 27th " | Received from War Office, Remount Circular No.45 re Branding of Horses with Broad Arrow. | I.A |
| 28th " | Request made to III Army for purchase of overalls for men dealing with verminous and contagious cases. | I.A |
| | Wire received from Practician (B/618) stating War Office require immediate report re rental arranged for STANSTED GLASSHOUSES hired for 2/5th F.A.Brigade. | I.A |
| | Wire 0/858 sent to Centreforce stating 100 Wagons required to complete Division. | I.A |
| 29th " | Letter from III Army,(7069/OS7 dated 29/12/15) advice of 8 - 5" Howitzers B.L. | I.A |
| | Wire received from III Army (OS/1062) stating NEW HUDSON cycles of Cyclist Coy will be inspected to-day by Experts as to suitability for oversea service. | |
| 30th " | Letter from III Army (7270/ST dated 30/12/15) stating arrangements for Supply & Transport at Artillery practice, LATCHINGDON PENINSULA, to be made by 61st (Sth.Mid.)Divn. | |
| | Wire from III Army (ST/256) stating 1/6th Field Coy.R.E. at BRIGHTLINGSEA will indent for rations on the 7th Provisional Brigade, GREAT BENTLEY. | I.A |
| | Secret letter to 179th Infantry Bde,(C/203Q/1i8) informing them re rations for Motor Bus Supply Column. | |
| 31st " | Letter from III Army (7105/OS) dated 31/12/15, stating 18 pr.QF received Stores approved. | I.A |
| | III Army letter,(WO.9/Arty/9243(A.2.) ammunition 18 pf. received complete 3600 rounds. | |
| | A.D.V.S. reports casualties during December, Horses dead or destroyed 12, cast & sold 91. | |

# WAR DIARY
## INTELLIGENCE SUMMARY.

General Staff.

Army Form C. 2118.

| Hour, Date, Place | Summary of Events and Information | Remarks and references to Appendices |
|---|---|---|
| 1915. December 1 | 1/2 no bounds of London Germany established Observation Post at HARLOW. | |
| | 5 men (1 each from Cyclists, Artillery, Infantry, A.S.C, & R.A.M.B.) proceeded to WOOLWICH for Farriery Course. | 80/- |
| 3 | 7 Officers (6 Infantry, 1 Cyclist) and 5 N.C.O's (4 Infantry, 1 Cyclist) proceeded to ONGAR for Engineering Course. | 80/- |
| | 3rd Army wire 3A/572/9 enclosing W.O. pamphlet A. 1877 as collection and transmission of intelligence received. | 80/- / 8M/- |
| 5 | 2 Officers proceeded to SHOEBURYNESS to attend Artillery Course. | 80/- |
| 6 | 3 Officers and 5 N.C.O's (Artillery) proceeded to DUNMOW for course of instruction in Signalling. | |
| | 1 Officer proceeded to LARK HILL to attend Artillery Course. | |
| | 5 Officers (4 Infantry, 1 Cyclist) and 9 N.C.O's (7 Infantry 2 Cyclists) proceeded to BISLEY for Musketry Course. | |
| | 12 men (6 Infantry 6 Cyclists) proceeded to WOOLWICH for course of instruction in Repair of Service Bicycles. | 80/- |
| Decr. 7/15. STANSTED ABBOTS | Observation Post established. | |
| | 2 Officers, A.S.C. proceeded to ALDERSHOT for A.S.C course. Instructions received from 3rd Army as Telegraphing "Nil" Intelligence Summaries. Also Instructions to extract W.O's letter 73/6614 (A.D.3). | 80/- |

Army Form C. 2118.

# WAR DIARY
## INTELLIGENCE SUMMARY.
*(Erase heading not required.)*

Instructions regarding War Diaries and Intelligence Summaries are contained in F.S. Regs., Part II. and the Staff Manual respectively. Title pages will be prepared in manuscript.

| Hour, Date, Place | Summary of Events and Information | Remarks and references to Appendices |
|---|---|---|
| December 9th | 1 Officer and 2 N.COs (Infantry) proceeded to GODSTONE to attend Grenadier Course. | SD/ |
| | 5 Officers and 10 N.COs (Infantry) proceeded to KELVEDON to attend 3rd Army Trench Fighting School. | |
| | 6 Officers (Infantry) proceeded to GIDEA PARK to attend Junior Officers' Course of Instruction. | SD/ |
| 10 | Lecture by Capt. A.G. PEMBERTON to 181st Infantry Brigade at BRAINTREE | SD/ |
| 11 | Capt. G.W. COLLIER, 7/13th Battalion London Regt. appointed Divisional Bombing Instructor, vice Captain CABUCHE | SD/ |
| BUNTINGFORD 13th 10.30 am | Brig. General inspected 11th Hants. Heavy Battery R.G.A. 3 Officers (Infantry) proceeded to OXTED to attend Junior Officers' Course of Instruction. | |
| | 2 Officers and 2 Warrant Officers (Infantry) proceeded to CHELSEA for Course of Instruction. | |
| | 4 Officers and 2 N.COs (Infantry) proceeded to BISLEY for Machine Gun Course. | |
| | Lecture by Divl. Machine Gun Officer to 119th Infantry Brigade at BISHOPS STORTFORD | SD/ |
| | New Intelligence Instructions (see 3rd instant) came into force. | |

# WAR DIARY

## INTELLIGENCE SUMMARY.

(Erase heading not required.)

Army Form C. 2118.

| Hour, Date, Place | Summary of Events and Information | Remarks and references to Appendices |
|---|---|---|
| December 14th | 1 N.C.O. and 8 men (Artillery) proceeded to ST ALBANS for Course of Instruction in Bombing. | |
| | Divisional Bombing School Staff assembled at Man[ ]nge STANSTED | |
| | Lieut. Colonel DUNLOP G.S.O.1, and Captain NAPIER conferred with O.C. 181st Infantry Brigade at BRAINTREE G.S.O.2, and afterwards visited 3rd Army Trench Fighting School at KELVEDON | SW |
| 15 | Lecture by Capt. A.G. PEMBERTON to 161st Infantry Brigade at STANSTED. | SW |
| 16 | Capt. NAPIER G.S.O.2, Capt. HALL G.S.O.3, Capt. PEMBERTON BRAINTREE and Lieut. WILSON YOUNG Divisional Machine Gun Officer, and Lieut. proceeded to GRANTHAM to visit Machine Gun Training Centre | |
| | 4 Officers, 6 N.C.Os and 60 men (Infantry) proceeded to STANSTED to attend Divisional Bombing Course. | SW |
| | 3rd Army approved 181st Infantry Brigade as "Emergency Brigade" | |
| 19 | Major General E.S. BULFIN assumes command of 60th (London) Division, vice Brigadier General CAYLEY | SW |

Army Form C. 2118.

# WAR DIARY
# of
# INTELLIGENCE SUMMARY.
(Erase heading not required.)

Instructions regarding War Diaries and Intelligence Summaries are contained in F.S. Regs., Part II. and the Staff Manual respectively. Title pages will be prepared in manuscript.

| Hour, Date, Place | Summary of Events and Information | Remarks and references to Appendices |
|---|---|---|
| December 20th | 5th Divisional Machine Gun Class and 11th Divisional Range-taking Course assembled at HADHAM HALL | |
| 9.30 a.m. BISHOPS STORTFORD | Lecture by Divisional Machine Gun Officer at BISHOPS STORTFORD | |
| 10.15 " | to 119th Infantry Brigade. | |
| 11.15 " SAWBRIDGEWORTH | | |
| 12.30 p.m. HATFIELD BROAD OAK | GENERAL OFFICER COMMANDING inspected units, as follows:- | |
| 2-0 p.m. HARLOW | 7/14 Battalion, London Regt. | |
| 3.30 p.m. " | 7/16 " " " | |
| 3.30 p.m. BISHOPS STORTFORD | 7/13 " " " | |
| | 60th (London) Divisional Cyclist Co. | |
| | 2/2nd County of London Yeomanry | |
| | A.L.C. Headquarter Co. | |
| | 119th Brigade Co. A.S.C. | |
| | | 8ay |
| December 21st | GENERAL OFFICER COMMANDING inspected the following Units:- | |
| 11 a.m. WARE | 7/15 Battalion, London Regt. | |
| | | 8ay |

# WAR DIARY
## of
## INTELLIGENCE SUMMARY.
(Erase heading not required.)

Army Form C. 2118.

| Hour, Date, Place | Summary of Events and Information | Remarks and references to Appendices |
|---|---|---|
| December 22nd | 8 Officers and 12 N.C.O.s (Yeomanry, R.E., and Infantry) proceeded to KELVEDON to attend 3rd Army Trench Fighting School. Lecture by Divisional Machine Gun Officer to 181st Infantry Brigade at BRAINTREE. GENERAL OFFICER COMMANDING inspected the following Units:- | |
| 9.30 a.m. STANSTED | 2/15th London Brigade, R.F.A. | |
| 10.0. a.m. " | 2/17th " " " | |
| 11.15 a.m. SAFFRON WALDEN | 2/19th Battalion, London Regt. | |
| 11.45 a.m. " | 2/19th " " | |
| 12.15 p.m. " | 2/18th " " | |
| 12.45 " " | No. 3 Company, A.S.C., "2/5th London Field Ambulance" and Brigade Headquarters Details | |
| 2.55 " HAVERHILL | 2/20th Battalion, London Regt. | |
| 11.45 a.m. BISHOPS STORTFORD | Brig. General ROPER inspected the following R.E. Units:- | SD/- |
| 12.30 p.m. STANSTED (Alan Meadow) | 2/4th London Field Coy. and "1/1st London Field Co. and also | |
| 1.15 p.m. BISHOPS STORTFORD | 3/3-0 Grange Stud Farm - Signal Coy. stables. | |
| 1.30 p.m. " | - Field Coy. stables | SD/- |

Army Form C. 2118.

# WAR DIARY
# INTELLIGENCE SUMMARY.
(Erase heading not required.)

Instructions regarding War Diaries and Intelligence Summaries are contained in F.S. Regs., Part II. and the Staff Manual respectively. Title pages will be prepared in manuscript.

| Hour, Date, Place | Summary of Events and Information | Remarks and references to Appendices |
|---|---|---|
| December 23 | GENERAL OFFICER COMMANDING inspected the following units:- | |
| 10.30 a.m. DUNMOW | 1/22nd Battalion, London Regt. | |
| 11.45 a.m. BRAINTREE | 1/6th (London) Divisional Signal Co., R.E. | |
| 12.0 noon " | 1/23rd Battalion, London Regt. | |
| 12.30 p.m. " | " | |
| 1.0 p.m. " | 1/24th " " | |
| 1.15 p.m. " | 1/6th London Field Ambulance. No. 4 Company, A.S.C. | |
| 2.45 p.m. COGGESHALL | 1/21st Battalion, London Regt. | SW/ |
| December 24 | GENERAL OFFICER COMMANDING inspected the following units:- | |
| 9.30 a.m. BISHOP'S STORTFORD | 1/4, 3/3rd and 1/6 London Field Companies, R.E. and 60th (London) Divisional Signal Co., R.E. | |
| 11.0 a.m. HADHAM STATION | 1/6 London Brigade, R.F.A. and Ammunition Column | |
| 12.0 noon STANDON | 1/8 London (Howitzer) Brigade, R.F.A. | |
| 12.45 p.m. BUNTINGFORD | 1/2nd London Heavy Battery, R.G.A. | |
| | Letter by Captain Bawkston (Divisional Machine Gun Officer) at Stafford Avenue to 180th Infantry Brigade. Telegram from Central Force conveying Christmas wishes from their Majesties The King and Queen Mary. | SW/ |

Army Form C. 2118.

# WAR DIARY
## or
## INTELLIGENCE SUMMARY.
(Erase heading not required.)

Instructions regarding War Diaries and Intelligence Summaries are contained in F.S. Regs., Part II. and the Staff Manual respectively. Title pages will be prepared in manuscript.

| Hour, Date, Place | Summary of Events and Information | Remarks and references to Appendices |
|---|---|---|
| December 25th | Instructions received by telegram from THIRD ARMY to proceed for three days to General Headquarters Expeditionary Force, France, on the 26th instant — | SM |
| December 27th | Second Divisional Bombing Course; assembled at Alsa Lodge, Bsh'd STANSTED | CAP |
| December 28th | GENERAL OFFICERS COMMANDING inspected :— | |
| 10.30 a.m. Maple Avenue, Bishops Stortford | No. 6 London Field Ambulance. | |
| 11.30 a.m. HADHAM HALL | Divisional Machine Gun School. | |
| 12.30 p.m. Clavel Hall ELSENHAM HALL | Divisional Clearing Hospital. | |
| | 3 N.C.O's (Infantry) 9 men 3-Infantry, 6-Cyclists) proceeded to WOOLWICH for Course of Instruction in Repair of Service Cycles | |
| | 3 Officers (Infantry) proceeded to CAMBRIDGE 6 men (Infantry) proceeded to BERMONDSEY for Junior Officers' Course. for Instruction in Cookery. | |
| | Lecture by Divisional Machine Gun Officer to 119th Infantry Brigade at Bishops Stortford BISHOPS STORTFORD | PM |

Army Form C. 2118.

# WAR DIARY
## INTELLIGENCE SUMMARY.
(Erase heading not required.)

Instructions regarding War Diaries and Intelligence Summaries are contained in F.S. Regs., Part II. and the Staff Manual respectively. Title pages will be prepared in manuscript.

| Hour, Date, Place | Summary of Events and Information | Remarks and references to Appendices |
|---|---|---|
| (continued) 28th December | 6 men (1 R.A. – 2, A.S.C. – 3, field ambce) proceeded to BERMONDSEY for course of Instruction in cold shoeing. | |
| | The undermentioned Officers reported to the EMBARKATION COMMANDANT SOUTHAMPTON at 4 p.m., preparatory to proceeding overseas for the purpose of temporary attachment to the British Army in the Field. | |
| | Col. E.W.D. BAIRD, Commdg. 179th Infantry Brigade | |
| | Col. G.H. TURNER, Commdg. 180th Infantry Brigade | |
| | Col. P.H. DALBIAC, Commdg. 60th (London) Divnl. Train | |
| | Lt. Col. R.Q. HENRIQUES, C.R.E. 60th (London) Division | |
| | Lt. Col. C.A. GORDON-CLARK, Commdg. 2/15th Bastn., London Regt. 7/19th. | |
| | Lt. Col. E.J. CHRISTIE, Commdg. " 2/19th " | |
| | Lt. Col. G.E. PYLE, Commdg. " 2/21st " | |
| | Major B. FLETCHER, Commdg. " 2/21st " | |
| 29th December | 2 N.C.Os (R.E.) proceeded to ALDERSHOT for course of Instruction in Secondary Duties. | |
| | Major General J.M.S. BRYNKER inspected Artillery Units Centre by Divisional Machine Gun Officer at BRAINTREE. | |
| 30th December 12-0 noon GOSFIELD | Inspection of Artillery Units by Major General BRYNKER & 181st Infantry Brigade continued. GENERAL OFFICER COMMANDING visited 181st Infantry Brigade during Brigade Exercise. | |

Army Form C. 2118.

# WAR DIARY
## INTELLIGENCE SUMMARY.
(Erase heading not required.)

| Hour, Date, Place | Summary of Events and Information | Remarks and references to Appendices |
|---|---|---|
| 31st December<br><br>Alba Rouge,<br>(STANSTED<br>SAFFRON WALDEN) | Inspection of Artillery by Major-General BRUNKER continued<br><br>GENERAL OFFICER COMMANDING inspected Divisional Bombing School<br><br>Lecture by Divisional Machine Gun Officer, to 180th Infantry Brigade.<br><br>Particulars of arrangements for Artillery Practice received from 3rd Army | 80/1 |

www.ingramcontent.com/pod-product-compliance
Lightning Source LLC
Chambersburg PA
CBHW081509160426
43193CB00014B/2635